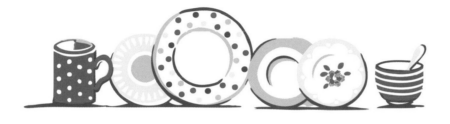

Cath Kidston®

MUG CAKES,
CUPCAKES & MORE

50 recipes for quick and easy sweet treats

quadrille

CONTENTS

....

INTRODUCTION

....

For those times when only a sweet treat will hit the spot, a delicious homemade cake must surely be top of everyone's wishlist. Whether you're baking for a coffee morning with friends, a post-lunch pick-me-up, an indulgent breakfast, a special afternoon tea or a family celebration, there's nothing more tempting than the smell of freshly baked cake.

For those occasions when only a sweet treat will do but time is at a premium, our mug cake recipes are the perfect solution. Next time you have a cake craving, grab your favourite mug, mix your ingredients and pop it in the microwave. It really is as simple as that! Unexpected visitors will be surprised and delighted when you offer them a freshly baked mug cake with their tea or coffee. And best of all, there's hardly any washing up!

Cupcakes are the perfect party cakes, especially if you choose colourful cupcake cases and display them on your best crockery. You'll find recipes for familiar favourites such as carrot, ginger and raspberry Bakewell cakes, as well as more unusual flavours like pistachio and pomegranate, toffee apple and lavender to try out.

For all the chocoholics out there, we have a chapter dedicated to all bakes chocolate, with easy recipes for brownies, mini cheesecakes, pavlovas and macaroons, plus new twists on chocolate classics like Black Forest gâteau and millionaire's shortbread.

No children's party would be complete without a special cake, so we've included some fun recipes for larger bakes – a train cake complete with engine, carriages and railway tracks, a bejewelled butterfly cake and an impressive-looking (but still easy to make) white chocolate rainbow cake with six colourful layers. These take a little more time, but are definitely worth the extra effort! And if you'd prefer smaller cakes for your little ones, we have lots of playful cupcake ideas that kids will love, from Snakes and Ladders party cupcakes to irresistible ice cream cupcakes complete with chocolate flakes and sprinkles.

We know that not everyone has time to spend hours baking and decorating (we certainly don't!), so we've made sure that all our recipes are clear and straightforward. They're aimed at the novice baker and you'll find plenty of tips and suggestions throughout. Let our pretty, modern vintage range of bakeware, china and fabrics inspire your presentation, decoration and choice of mug; serve your bakes piled high and gather your guests round for a proper celebration.

MUG
CAKES

MUG CAKES

....

What could be simpler than making a cake in a mug?
If it sounds too good to be true, give it a try! Quick, easy
and convenient, all of our recipes can be made from
scratch in only a few minutes.

Start the day with a warming banana, oat and honey breakfast mug
cake or go for an indulgent chocolate marshmallow mug cake for
one. These super-speedy cakes are perfect for last-minute visitors,
satisfying a sudden craving for something sweet and for days when
you are short on time and only cake will do! Your microwave isn't
just for heating leftovers and meals for one – put it to good use and
find out why mug cakes have become so popular.

Most of the recipes are designed to be served straight
from the mug, meaning minimal washing up and
a new lease of life for your favourite mug!

RHUBARB CRUMBLE AND CUSTARD MUG CAKE

SERVES 1

For the topping
2 tsp rolled oats
2 tsp unsalted butter
3 tsp plain (all-purpose) flour
2 tsp caster (superfine) sugar

For the rhubarb
1 tsp unsalted butter, plus extra for greasing
100g (1 cup) rhubarb, chopped into 2cm (¾in) pieces
1 tbsp caster (superfine) sugar
1 tsp juice and finely grated zest of ½ clementine

For the cake
30g (2 tbsp) unsalted butter, softened
1 medium free-range egg
1 tbsp milk
½ tsp vanilla extract
3 tbsp golden caster (superfine) sugar
4 tbsp self-raising flour

warm custard, to serve

Preheat the oven to 180°C/350°F/gas 4. Start by making the topping. Rub together all the topping ingredients with your fingertips until the mixture forms little clumps. Tip the crumble onto a small, shallow baking tray and bake for 4–5 minutes, or until golden and crisp. Keep an eye on it though, and make sure you shake the tray occasionally to ensure the crumble cooks evenly. Set aside.

Lightly grease a 350ml (12fl oz) mug and set aside. Place the butter, rhubarb, sugar and clementine juice and zest into a separate mug and cook for 2 minutes 20 seconds at 600W, 2 minutes at 800W or 1 minute 40 seconds at 1000W (or until tender). Drain the excess liquid and tip into the greased mug. Reserve a spoonful of rhubarb to spoon on top of the cooked cake before serving. Wash out the mug the rhubarb was cooked in.

Recipe continues overleaf

To make the cake, add the butter to the cleaned mug and microwave for 10–20 seconds, or until melted. Add the egg, milk and vanilla extract and beat with a fork until combined. Add the sugar and flour and beat together.

Pour the cake mixture over the rhubarb. Cook in the microwave for 2 minutes 20 seconds at 600W, 2 minutes at 800W or 1 minute 40 seconds at 1000W. Place the reserved spoonful of rhubarb on top of the cake.

Scatter over the crumble topping and serve hot with warm custard.

VARIATION

To keep rhubarb fresh, store the stalks in the fridge with the leaves intact. This will prevent it from wilting and help it to stay fresh for longer.

BANANA, OAT AND HONEY BREAKFAST MUG CAKE

SERVES 1

1 small/medium (about 100g/3½oz) ripe banana

1 tbsp sunflower or light olive oil

1 medium egg

1 tbsp milk

2 tbsp runny honey, plus extra to serve

2 tbsp muscovado sugar

3 tbsp self-raising flour

pinch ground cinnamon, plus extra to serve

1 tbsp rolled oats

1 tbsp sultanas (golden raisins)

natural Greek yoghurt, to serve

Mash three-quarters of the banana (reserve the rest for later) and tip it into a 350ml (12fl oz) mug. Add the oil, egg, milk and honey, and mix together with a fork. Stir in the sugar, flour, cinnamon, oats and sultanas, mixing together well.

Cook in the microwave for 3 minutes 20 seconds at 600W, 3 minutes at 800W or 2 minutes 40 seconds at 1000W.

Remove the mug from the microwave and leave to cool for a few minutes before topping with a dollop of yoghurt, a few slices of the reserved banana, a drizzle of honey and a dusting of cinnamon to serve.

CHOCOLATE MARSHMALLOW MUG CAKE

SERVES 1

30g (2 tbsp) unsalted butter, softened, plus extra for greasing

40g (¼ cup) good-quality dark (bitter-sweet) chocolate (70 per cent cocoa solids), chopped

1 medium egg

1 tbsp milk

2 tbsp light muscovado sugar

3 tbsp self-raising flour

1 tbsp mini marshmallows

20g (⅛ cup) milk and white chocolate drops

3 large marshmallows

Lightly grease a 350ml (12fl oz) mug and set aside.

Place the butter and chocolate into a separate mug and microwave for 20 seconds, or until melted. Add the egg and milk and beat with a fork until combined. Add the sugar, flour and mini marshmallows and the chocolate drops (reserving a few for later) and fold together. Spoon into the greased mug and smooth the surface with the back of a spoon.

Cook in the microwave for 2 minutes 50 seconds at 600W, 2 minutes 30 seconds at 800W or 2 minutes 10 seconds at 1000W. Remove the mug from the microwave.

Scatter the large marshmallows over the top and place under a hot grill for 30 seconds, or until melted and just turning golden. Scatter with the reserved chocolate drops and serve hot.

STICKY TOFFEE PUDDING MUG CAKE

30g (2 tbsp) salted butter, plus extra for greasing

2 tbsp salted caramel sauce

1 medium egg

2 tsp treacle (blackstrap molasses)

1 tsp stem ginger syrup

½ ball stem ginger, chopped

1 tsp caramel extract

30g (⅛ cup) Medjool dates, pitted and chopped

3 tbsp dark muscovado sugar

4 tbsp self-raising flour

¼ tsp ground ginger

whipped cream, to serve

Lightly grease a 350ml (12fl oz) mug with butter, then pour 1 tbsp of salted caramel sauce into the bottom of the mug. Place the butter in a separate mug and microwave for 20 seconds, or until melted. Add the egg, treacle, ginger syrup, chopped stem ginger, caramel extract and dates, and whisk together with a small whisk.

Stir in the sugar, flour and ground ginger, and beat again until smooth. Spoon the mixture over the top of the caramel sauce. Cook in the microwave for 2 minutes 20 seconds at 600W, 2 minutes at 800W or 1 minute 40 seconds at 1000W.

Serve hot with a dollop of whipped cream and the remaining caramel sauce.

GRANOLA MUG CAKE

SERVES 1

For the topping	*For the cake*
2 tbsp rolled oats	2 tbsp unsalted butter, softened
1 tsp flaked almonds	1 medium egg
1 tsp maple syrup or runny honey	1 tbsp milk
1 tsp light oil, plus extra for oiling	2 tbsp caster (superfine) sugar
	1 tbsp runny honey
For the compote	3 tbsp ground almonds
unsalted butter, for greasing	3 tbsp self-raising flour
50g (¼ cup) mixed berries, such as blueberries, blackberries and raspberries	½ tsp vanilla extract
1 tsp runny honey or maple syrup	mixed berries, natural yoghurt and
¼ tsp vanilla extract	runny honey, to serve

Start by making the topping. Preheat the oven to 180°C/350°F/gas 4. Mix together the oats, flaked almonds, maple syrup and oil and spread out over a lightly oiled baking tray. Bake for 5 minutes, or until pale golden and crisp. Remove from the oven and set aside.

Lightly grease a 350ml (12fl oz) mug. To make the compote, mix the berries, honey and vanilla extract together, and place in the mug.

For the cakes, place the butter in a separate mug and microwave for 20 seconds, or until melted. Add the egg, milk, sugar, honey and vanilla extract and beat with a fork until combined.

Recipe continues overleaf

Fold in the ground almonds and flour, then spoon over the top of the compote in the greased mug.

Cook in the microwave for 2 minutes 50 seconds at 600W, 2 minutes 30 seconds at 800W or 2 minutes 10 seconds at 1000W. Remove the mug from the microwave. Scatter the granola topping over the top, and add a few mixed berries, a dollop of natural yoghurt and a drizzle of honey before serving.

TIP

It is lovely to use orange blossom honey if you can find it as it adds a delicious citrus flavour, but you can just as easily use regular runny honey if you prefer.

CHERRY AND ALMOND CHRISTMAS MUG CAKE

SERVES 1

For the cake

15g (1 tbsp) unsalted butter, softened, plus extra for greasing

1½ tbsp fresh orange or clementine juice

45g (⅓ cup) sultanas (golden raisins)

1 tbsp each of dried cherries, chopped dried apricots and soft prunes

1 medium egg

3 tbsp dark muscovado sugar

1 tsp treacle (blackstrap molasses)

½ clementine, finely grated zest

1 tbsp self-raising flour

10g (1 tbsp) toasted hazelnuts, roughly chopped

10g (1 tbsp) toasted almonds, roughly chopped

¼ tsp mixed spice

¼ tsp ground ginger

To decorate

icing (powdered) sugar, to dust

75g (¼ cup) ready-to-roll marzipan

2 tsp apricot jam

75g (¼ cup) ready-to-roll white fondant icing

50g (⅔ cup) powdered fondant icing sugar

gold ribbon

edible silver stars, snowflakes and glitter, and Christmas cake decorations

Lightly grease a 350ml (12fl oz) cappuccino mug and set aside.

Place the butter, orange juice, sultanas and dried fruit in a separate mug and microwave for 30 seconds, or until the butter is melted and the fruit has plumped up. Add the egg, sugar, treacle and clementine zest and beat with a fork until combined. Stir in the flour, nuts and spices and spoon into the greased mug.

Recipe continues overleaf

Cover with clingfilm (plastic wrap). Cook in the microwave for 3 minutes 20 seconds at 600W, 3 minutes at 800W or 2 minutes 40 seconds at 1000W. Remove the mug from the microwave and leave to cool for at least 10 minutes.

Run a small palette knife around the edges of the mug to loosen the cake, then invert it onto a plate. Leave to cool completely.

Now move on to the decorations. Lightly dust the work surface with icing sugar and roll out the marzipan to 5mm (¼in) thick. Spread the cake with a thin even layer of jam, then place the marzipan over the top. Smooth the edges flat with your hands so that the cake is evenly covered, then trim the bottom off with a sharp knife.

Lightly dust the work surface with a little more icing sugar and roll out the ready-to-roll fondant icing to 5mm (¼in) thick. Brush the marzipan with a little more apricot jam, then layer the fondant icing over the top. Smooth the edges flat with your hands so that the cake is evenly covered, then trim off the bottom with a sharp knife.

Place the powdered fondant icing sugar in a bowl, stir in 1 tsp of cold water or enough to make a thick paste, then dribble over the top of the cake to look like snow. Secure a gold ribbon around the edge of the cake and seal with double-sided sticky tape or pins. Decorate the top with edible silver stars, snowflakes and glitter, and Christmas cake decorations.

MOLTEN MIDDLE HAZELNUT CHOCOLATE MUG CAKE

SERVES 1

30g salted butter, softened, plus extra for greasing

40g (¼ cup) good-quality dark (bitter-sweet) chocolate (70 per cent cocoa solids), finely chopped

1 medium egg

2 tbsp milk

2 tbsp golden caster (superfine) sugar

1 tbsp soft brown sugar

3 tbsp self-raising flour

2 tsp chocolate spread

10g (1 tbsp) toasted hazelnuts, roughly chopped

Lightly grease a 350ml (12fl oz) mug and set aside.

Place the butter and chocolate in a separate mug and microwave for 20 seconds, or until melted. Beat in the egg and milk with a fork. Add both sugars and the flour and beat until combined. Pour into the greased mug. Place 1 tsp of the chocolate spread on top of the cake (reserve the rest for later).

Cook in the microwave for 2 minutes 20 seconds at 600W, 2 minutes at 800W or 1 minute 40 seconds at 1000W.

Remove the mug from the microwave. Place the remaining spoonful of chocolate spread on top of the cake, scatter with the toasted hazelnuts and serve warm.

CHOCOLATE TOFFEE FUDGE MUG CAKE

SERVES 1

30g (2 tbsp) unsalted butter, softened, plus extra for greasing

2 tbsp salted caramel sauce

40g (¼ cup) good-quality dark (bitter-sweet) chocolate (70 per cent cocoa solids), finely chopped

1 medium egg

1 tbsp milk

1 tsp caramel extract

2 tbsp light muscovado sugar

3 tbsp self-raising flour

20g (¾oz) fudge, cut into small pieces

Lightly grease a 350ml (12fl oz) mug and pour 1 tbsp of the caramel sauce into the base.

Place the butter and chocolate in a separate mug and microwave for 20 seconds, or until melted. Add the egg, milk and caramel extract, and beat with a fork until combined. Add the sugar, flour and fudge (reserving 1 tbsp for later), and fold together. Spoon into the greased mug on top of the caramel sauce and smooth the surface with the back of a spoon.

Cook in the microwave for 3 minutes 20 seconds at 600W, 3 minutes at 800W or 2 minutes 40 seconds at 1000W.

Remove the mug from the microwave. Spoon the remaining caramel sauce over the top of the warm cake, scatter with the reserved fudge and serve hot.

(pictured left overleaf)

PEANUT BUTTER JELLY FONDANT MUG CAKE

SERVES 2

30g (2 tbsp) salted butter, softened, plus extra for greasing

40g (¼ cup) good-quality dark (bitter-sweet) chocolate (70 per cent cocoa solids), finely chopped

1 medium egg

2 tbsp milk

2 tbsp golden caster (superfine) sugar

1 tbsp soft brown sugar

4 tbsp self-raising flour

4 tsp raspberry jam

4 tsp peanut butter

fresh raspberries, to serve

Lightly grease 2 x 250ml (8¾fl oz) mugs and set aside.

Place the butter and chocolate in a separate mug and microwave for 20 seconds, or until melted. Beat in the egg and milk with a fork. Add both sugars and the flour and beat until combined. Divide half of the mixture evenly between the mugs, reserving the other half. Place 1 tsp of jam and 1 tsp of peanut butter on top of each cake, then divide the remaining cake mixture between the mugs. Smooth the tops with the back of a spoon.

Cook in the microwave for 2 minutes 20 seconds at 600W, 2 minutes at 800W or 1 minute 40 seconds at 1000W.

Remove the mugs from the microwave and leave to cool for 2 minutes. Run a small palette knife around the edges of the mugs to loosen the cakes, then invert them onto plates.

Place the remaining raspberry jam and peanut butter on top of each fondant, scatter fresh raspberries around the plates and serve.

(pictured right overleaf)

RASPBERRY, ROSE AND COCONUT MUG CAKE

SERVES 1

30g (2 tbsp) unsalted butter, softened

1 medium egg

½–1 tsp rosewater, to taste

4 tbsp caster (superfine) sugar

3 tbsp desiccated coconut, toasted

3 tbsp self-raising flour

40g (⅓ cup) raspberries, plus extra to serve

toasted coconut flakes, to serve

icing (powdered) sugar, to dust

Place the butter in a 350ml (12fl oz) mug and microwave for 20 seconds, or until melted. Add the egg, rosewater and caster sugar and beat until combined. Add the desiccated coconut and flour and beat until combined. Stir in the raspberries.

Cook in the microwave for 2 minutes 50 seconds at 600W, 2 minutes 30 seconds at 800W or 2 minutes 10 seconds at 1000W.

Remove the mug from the microwave. Scatter with extra raspberries and coconut flakes. Decorate with a dusting of icing sugar.

(pictured overleaf)

ORANGE AND POPPY SEED MUG CAKE

SERVES 1

For the cake

30g (2 tbsp) unsalted butter, softened, plus extra for greasing

1 medium egg

1 tbsp orange juice and finely grated zest of ½ orange, plus extra, to decorate

3 tbsp caster (superfine) sugar

4 tbsp self-raising flour

½ tsp poppy seeds

For the buttercream

15g (1 tbsp) unsalted butter, softened

30g (¼ cup) icing (powdered) sugar

1 tsp orange juice

Lightly grease a 350ml (12fl oz) mug with butter and set aside.

To make the cake, place the butter in a separate mug and microwave for 10 seconds, or until melted. Add the egg and orange juice and zest and beat with a fork until combined. Add the sugar, flour and poppy seeds and beat until smooth. Spoon into the greased mug and smooth the surface with the back of a spoon.

Cook in the microwave for 2 minutes 10 seconds at 600W, 1 minute 50 seconds at 800W or 1 minute 30 seconds at 1000W. Set aside to cool.

For the buttercream, beat together the butter and icing sugar, then fold in the orange juice.

Spoon the icing into a piping bag fitted with a star nozzle and pipe the icing on top of the cooled cake. Decorate with orange zest before serving.

(pictured overleaf)

POACHED PEAR AND ALMOND MUG CAKE

SERVES 1

30g (2 tbsp) unsalted butter, softened

1 medium egg

1 tbsp milk

1 tsp almond extract

3 tbsp light muscovado sugar

3 tbsp ground almonds

3 tbsp self-raising flour

1 ripe pear, peeled

½ tbsp flaked almonds, toasted

Place the butter in a 350ml (12fl oz) mug and microwave for 20 seconds, or until melted.

Add the egg, milk, almond extract and sugar and beat with a fork until smooth. Add the ground almonds and flour and beat until combined. Halve the pear lengthways (leaving the stalk intact), remove the core and place one half into the cake mixture. Chop one-quarter of the remaining pear half and scatter around the top of the mug. Scatter over the flaked almonds. Cook in the microwave for 2 minutes 30 seconds at 600W, 2 minutes 10 seconds at 800W or 1 minute 50 seconds at 1000W.

Remove the mug from the microwave and serve.

CUPCAKES

CUPCAKES

....

Deceptively easy to bake, cupcakes are a real winner if you're looking to impress, whatever the occasion. Bake them for party guests, win over work colleagues and serve on a pretty cake stand at a coffee morning or tea party.

Once you've chosen your recipe and mixed up your ingredients, choose colourful cases to bake your cupcakes in and have fun perfecting your icing and decoration. These simple recipes for indulgent morsels all have one thing in common – the perfect combination of moist, light cake and sweet, fluffy icing. So whether you're looking for fresh, fruity cakes for a summer party or rich ginger cakes to go with a pot of freshly brewed tea, there's a cupcake here for everyone.

STRAWBERRY AND WHITE CHOCOLATE CUPCAKES

MAKES 12

For the cakes

125g (½ cup, plus 1 tbsp) unsalted butter, softened

125g (⅔ cup, minus 2 tsp) golden caster (superfine) sugar

2 large eggs

125g (1 cup) self-raising flour

1 tsp baking powder

1 tsp vanilla extract

1–2 tbsp milk

50g (⅓ cup) white chocolate, cut into small chunks

100g (¾ cup) strawberries, hulled and chopped into small pieces

1 tbsp freeze-dried strawberry pieces

¼ tsp red gel colouring

To decorate

100g (⅔ cup) white chocolate, chopped

150g (⅔ cup) unsalted butter, softened

140g (1 cup, plus 3 tbsp) icing (powdered) sugar, sifted

1–2 tbsp milk

1 tbsp freeze-dried strawberry pieces and a few fresh strawberries, quartered

Preheat the oven to 180°C/350°F/gas 4. Line a 12-hole muffin tin with paper cupcake cases.

To make the cakes, place the butter and sugar in a large bowl and beat with an electric whisk until pale and fluffy. Add the eggs, one at a time, beating well between each addition. Sift over the flour and baking powder and fold in using a large metal spoon. Add the vanilla extract and milk. Spoon half the mixture into a separate bowl and stir in the chocolate.

Recipe continues overleaf

Place the strawberries into a small blender and whizz to a smooth purée. Fold 2 tbsp of the strawberry purée (reserving the rest for the icing) into the mixture without the chocolate, and also stir in the freeze-dried strawberry pieces. Add the tip of a knife coated with red gel colouring to the strawberry mix and fold through.

Divide the strawberry mixture evenly between the paper cases and smooth the tops with the back of a spoon. Spoon the white chocolate mixture over the top of each cake to make two layers and smooth the tops with the back of a spoon. Bake for 18 minutes, or until well risen and slightly springy to the touch. Remove the cakes from the tin and transfer to a wire rack to cool.

Meanwhile, make the icing. Place the chocolate in a microwavable bowl and melt in 30-second bursts in the microwave, stirring between each burst. Alternatively, place the chocolate in a small bowl that fits snugly over a pan of gently simmering water and leave for a few minutes to melt.

Beat the butter and icing sugar in a large bowl with an electric whisk until pale and fluffy, then fold in the melted chocolate. Beat in enough milk so that the mix is light and fluffy. Gently fold 3 tbsp of the reserved strawberry purée into the icing, but don't fold it in completely as you want a colourful swirled effect. Spoon the icing into a piping bag fitted with a star nozzle.

When the cupcakes are cool, pipe the icing onto the top of each cake and scatter with the fresh and freeze-dried strawberry pieces.

TIP

Freeze-dried strawberry pieces are available in large supermarkets, in the baking section. They really intensify the strawberry flavour of these cupcakes.

BLUEBERRY AND ALMOND CUPCAKES

MAKES 12

125g (½ cup, plus 1 tbsp) unsalted butter, softened

125g (⅔ cup, minus 2 tsp) golden caster (superfine) sugar

2 large eggs

75g (½ cup, plus ½ tbsp) self-raising flour

1½ tsp baking powder

50g (½ cup) ground almonds

2½ tsp almond extract

100g (¾ cup) blueberries

1–2 tbsp milk

200g (1½ cups, minus 1 tbsp) fondant icing sugar

Preheat the oven to 180°C/350°F/gas 4. Line a 12-hole muffin tin with paper cupcake cases.

To make the cakes, place the butter and sugar in a large bowl and beat with an electric whisk until pale and fluffy. Add the eggs, one at a time, beating well between each addition. Sift over the flour and baking powder then fold in using a large metal spoon. Fold in the ground almonds, 1 teaspoon of the almond extract, most of the blueberries (reserving 12 for decoration) and enough milk for the mixture to be of a dropping consistency.

Divide the mixture evenly between the paper cases and smooth the tops with the back of a spoon. Bake for 18 minutes, or until well risen and slightly springy to the touch.

Place the fondant icing sugar in a large bowl, add 1–2 tbsp of cold water and the remaining almond extract and beat until combined to a spoonable icing. Add a little more water if the icing is too stiff.

Spoon the icing over each of the cooled cakes and top with a reserved blueberry before serving.

VANILLA VERY BERRY CUPCAKES

MAKES 12

For the cakes	To decorate
125g (½ cup, plus 1 tbsp) unsalted butter, softened	100g (⅔ cup) white chocolate, chopped, plus extra, grated
125g (⅔ cup, minus 2 tsp) golden caster (superfine) sugar	150g (⅔ cup) unsalted butter, softened
2 large eggs	140g (1 cup, plus 3 tbsp) icing (powdered) sugar, sifted
125g (1 cup) self-raising flour	1–2 tbsp milk
1 tsp baking powder	fresh raspberries
1 tsp vanilla extract	1 tbsp freeze-dried raspberry pieces
100g (¾ cup) fresh raspberries	
2 tsp freeze-dried raspberry pieces	
1–2 tbsp milk	

Preheat the oven to 180°C/350°F/gas 4. Line a 12-hole muffin tin with paper cupcake cases.

Place the butter and sugar in a large bowl and beat with an electric whisk until pale and fluffy. Add the eggs, one at a time, beating between each addition. Sift over the flour and baking powder and fold in using a metal spoon. Add the vanilla extract, the fresh and freeze-dried berries and enough milk for the mixture to be of a dropping consistency.

Divide the mixture evenly between the paper cases and smooth with the back of a spoon. Bake for 18 minutes, or until well risen and springy to the touch. Remove the cakes from the tin and transfer to a wire rack to cool.

To make the icing, place the chocolate in a bowl and melt in 30-second bursts in the microwave, stirring between each burst. Beat the butter and icing sugar in a bowl with an electric whisk until pale and fluffy. Fold in the melted chocolate and the milk. Spoon the icing into a piping bag fitted with a star nozzle. When the cakes are cool, pipe the icing onto the tops and scatter with a fresh berry, freeze-dried berries and grated white chocolate.

BANOFFEE CUPCAKES

MAKES 12

For the cakes

125g (½ cup, plus 1 tbsp) salted butter, softened, plus extra for greasing

125g (⅔ cup) light muscovado sugar

2 large eggs, lightly beaten

150g (1 cup, plus 2 tbsp) self-raising flour, plus extra for dusting

1 tsp baking powder

2 medium ripe bananas, mashed

75g (2½oz) vanilla fudge, cut into small cubes

To decorate

150g (⅔ cup) salted butter

225g (2 cups, minus 1 tbsp) icing (powdered) sugar

75g (2½oz) toffee caramel sauce

1 banana, sliced

Preheat the oven to 180°C/350°F/gas 4. Line a 12-hole muffin tin with paper cupcake cases.

To make the cakes, place the butter and sugar in a large bowl and beat for about 5 minutes with an electric whisk until light and fluffy. Add the eggs, one at a time, beating well between each addition. Add the flour, baking powder, mashed bananas and fudge (saving a small handful of fudge for decorating).

Divide the mixture evenly between the paper cases and smooth the tops with the back of a spoon. Bake for 18 minutes, or until well risen and golden and slightly springy to the touch. Transfer the cakes to a wire rack to cool.

Meanwhile, make the icing. Beat together the butter, icing sugar and caramel sauce until smooth. Spoon the icing into a piping bag fitted with a star nozzle and pipe onto each cake. Scatter with the reserved fudge and banana slices and serve.

STRAWBERRY CHEESECAKE CUPCAKES

For the cakes

125g (½ cup, plus 1 tbsp) unsalted butter, softened

125g (⅔ cup, minus 2 tsp) golden caster sugar

2 large eggs

125g (1 cup) self-raising flour

1 tsp baking powder

½ orange, finely grated zest

2 tbsp milk

100g (¾ cup) strawberries, hulled and chopped into small pieces

To decorate

50g (3½ tbsp) unsalted butter, softened

150g (¾ cup) cream cheese, at room temperature

4 tbsp icing (powdered) sugar

1 vanilla pod (bean), seeds scraped out

½ ginger biscuit, crushed into crumbs

12 strawberries, halved or sliced

Preheat the oven to 180°C/350°F/gas 4. Line a 12-hole muffin tin with paper cupcake cases.

To make the cakes, place the butter and sugar in a bowl and beat with an electric whisk until pale and fluffy. Add the eggs, one at a time, beating well between each addition. Sift over the flour and baking powder. Fold in with a metal spoon. Add the orange zest, milk and strawberries and fold together.

Divide the mixture evenly between the paper cases and smooth the tops with the back of a spoon. Bake for 18 minutes, or until well risen and slightly springy to the touch. Remove the cakes from the tin and transfer to a wire rack to cool.

To make the icing, beat together the butter, cream cheese, icing sugar and vanilla seeds until smooth.

When the cupcakes are cool, use a palette knife to spread the icing onto each cake. Scatter with the biscuit crumbs, arrange a strawberry on top of each and serve immediately.

PINEAPPLE, COCONUT AND LIME CUPCAKES

MAKES 12

For the cakes

40g (½ cup) desiccated coconut

125g (½ cup, plus 1 tbsp) unsalted butter, softened

125g (⅔ cup) golden caster (superfine) sugar

2 large eggs

85g (⅔ cup) self-raising flour

1½ tsp baking powder

50g (¼ cup) fresh or tinned pineapple, chopped

1 lime, finely grated zest

2 tbsp coconut milk or cow's milk

To decorate

200g (¾ cup plus 2 tbsp) unsalted butter, softened

350g (2½ cups) icing (powdered) sugar

½ lime, grated zest and 2 tbsp juice

Preheat the oven to 180°C/350°F/gas 4. Line a 12-hole muffin tin with paper cupcake cases.

Place the desiccated coconut in a dry frying pan and toast over a low heat for 2 minutes, until lightly golden. Remove from the heat and leave to cool.

Place the butter and sugar in a bowl and beat with an electric whisk until pale and fluffy. Add the eggs, one at a time, beating between each addition. Sift over the flour and baking powder. Fold in using a metal spoon. Set aside 1 tbsp toasted coconut. Add the remaining toasted coconut, the pineapple and lime zest to the mix and fold in. Stir in the coconut or cow's milk. Divide the mixture between the paper cases and smooth the tops with the back of a spoon. Bake for 18 minutes, or until well risen and springy to the touch. Remove the cakes from the tin and transfer to a wire rack to cool.

For the icing, beat the butter and icing sugar together in a large bowl with an electric whisk until pale and fluffy. Add the lime zest and juice, reserving a little zest for decorating, and beat until combined. Spoon into a piping bag fitted with a star nozzle. When the cakes are cool, pipe icing onto each cake and scatter with the reserved toasted coconut and lime zest before serving.

LEMON MERINGUE CUPCAKES

MAKES 12

For the cakes

125g (½ cup, plus 1 tbsp) unsalted butter, softened

125g (⅔ cup, minus 2 tsp) caster (superfine) sugar

2 large eggs

125g (1 cup) self-raising flour

1½ tsp baking powder

1 lemon, finely grated zest and 1–2 tbsp juice

4 tbsp lemon curd

For the meringue topping

2 large egg whites

100g (½ cup) caster (superfine) sugar

1 tsp cornflour (cornstarch)

1 tsp vanilla extract

Preheat the oven to 180°C/350°F/gas 4. Line a 12-hole muffin tin with paper cupcake cases.

To make the cakes, place the butter and sugar in a bowl and beat with an electric whisk until pale and fluffy. Add the eggs, one at a time, beating well between each addition. Sift over the flour and baking powder and fold in using a metal spoon. Add the lemon zest and juice and fold together.

Divide the mixture evenly between the paper cases and smooth the tops with the back of a spoon. Bake for 18 minutes, or until well risen and slightly springy to the touch. Remove the cakes from the tin and transfer to a wire rack to cool. Put the lemon curd into a piping bag fitted with a straight nozzle, take a scoop out of each cake and pipe 1 tsp of curd into each cake.

Prepare the meringue topping. Place the egg whites in a bowl and whisk with an electric whisk until they form firm peaks. Add the sugar, 1 tbsp at a time, and whisk continuously until the mixture is glossy and stiff. Whisk in the cornflour and vanilla extract. Spoon the meringue into a piping bag fitted with a star nozzle and pipe onto the cooled cakes.

Place the cakes back in the oven and bake for 10–12 minutes, or until the meringue is lightly golden and crisp. Serve warm or at room temperature.

(pictured left overleaf)

ETON MESS CUPCAKES

MAKES 12

For the cakes

125g (½ cup, plus 1 tbsp) unsalted butter, softened

125g (⅔ cup, minus 2 tsp) golden caster (superfine) sugar

2 large eggs

125g (1 cup) self-raising flour

1 tsp baking powder

1 tsp vanilla extract

2 tbsp milk

50g (⅓ cup) strawberries, hulled

To decorate

250ml (1 cup) double (heavy) cream

2 tbsp icing (powdered) sugar

1 tsp vanilla extract

75g (½ cup) strawberries, chopped

20g mini meringues

Preheat the oven to 180°C/350°F/gas 4. Line a 12-hole muffin tin with paper cupcake cases.

To make the cakes, place the butter and sugar in a large bowl and beat with an electric whisk until pale and fluffy. Add the eggs, one at a time, beating well between each addition. Sift over the flour and baking powder and fold in, along with the vanilla extract and milk, using a large metal spoon.

Tip the strawberries into a blender and blend to make a purée. Lightly swirl 4 tbsp of the purée into the cake mixture, leaving a rippled effect. Divide the mixture between the paper cases and smooth the tops with the back of a spoon. Bake for 18 minutes, or until well risen and springy to the touch. Remove the cakes from the tin and transfer to a wire rack to cool.

Meanwhile, make the icing. Whip the cream with the icing sugar and vanilla extract until the mixture forms soft peaks. Spoon the icing into a piping bag fitted with a star nozzle.

When the cupcakes are cool, pipe the icing on top of the cakes, drizzle with a little of the remaining strawberry purée, and scatter with the chopped strawberries and mini meringues. Serve immediately.

(pictured right overleaf)

RASPBERRY BAKEWELL CUPCAKES

For the cakes	To decorate
125g (½ cup, plus 1 tbsp) unsalted butter, softened	200g (1½ cups, minus 1 tbsp) fondant icing sugar
125g (⅔ cup, minus 2 tsp) golden caster (superfine) sugar	2 tbsp lemon juice, plus a little extra if needed
2 large eggs	12 fresh raspberries
75g (½ cup, plus ½ tbsp) self-raising flour	15g (1 tbsp) flaked almonds, lightly toasted
1½ tsp baking powder	
50g (½ cup) ground almonds	
1 tsp almond extract	
1–2 tbsp milk	
3 tbsp raspberry jam	

Preheat the oven to 180°C/350°F/gas 4. Line a 12-hole muffin tin with paper cupcake cases.

To make the cakes, place the butter and sugar in a large bowl and beat with an electric whisk until pale and fluffy. Add the eggs, one at a time, beating between each addition. Sift over the flour and baking powder and fold in using a metal spoon. Fold in the ground almonds, almond extract and enough milk for the mixture to be of a dropping consistency.

Divide the mixture evenly between the paper cases and smooth the tops with the back of a spoon. Bake for 18 minutes, or until well risen and springy to the touch. Remove from the tin and cool on a wire rack. Take a scoop out of the middle of each cake and fill with 1 tsp of jam.

To make the icing, place the fondant icing sugar in a bowl, add 2 tbsp of lemon juice and beat until combined to a pourable consistency. Add a little more lemon juice if it is too stiff. Spoon over the cooled cakes, place a raspberry in the middle of each and decorate with flaked almonds.

TOFFEE APPLE CUPCAKES

MAKES 12

For the cakes

125g (½ cup, plus 1 tbsp) salted butter, softened, plus extra for greasing

125g (⅔ cup) light muscovado sugar

2 large eggs

125g (1 cup) self-raising flour

2 tsp baking powder

½ tsp ground cinnamon

½ tsp ground ginger

1 apple (about 100g/3½oz), peeled, cored and cut into small cubes

1–2 tbsp apple juice

To decorate

150g (⅔ cup) unsalted butter, softened

225g (about 1⅔ cups) icing (powdered) sugar

75g (2½oz) toffee caramel sauce

pinch ground cinnamon

50g (2oz) hard toffees, bashed into small pieces

edible gold sugar

Preheat the oven to 180°C/350°F/gas 4. Line a 12-hole muffin tin with paper cupcake cases.

To make the cakes, place the butter and sugar in a large bowl and beat until pale and fluffy. Add the eggs, one at a time, beating well between each addition. Sift over the flour, baking powder and spices, and fold in with the apple. Fold in enough apple juice for the mixture to be of a dropping consistency.

Divide the mixture evenly between the paper cases and smooth the tops with the back of a spoon. Bake for 18 minutes, or until well risen, pale golden and springy to the touch. Remove the cakes from the tin and place on a wire rack to cool.

Recipe continues overleaf

Meanwhile, make the icing. Place the butter and icing sugar in a large bowl and beat with an electric whisk until pale and fluffy. Beat in the toffee caramel sauce and cinnamon. Spoon the icing into a piping bag fitted with a star nozzle and pipe a swirl of icing onto each cake. Decorate with the toffee pieces and a sprinkling of edible sugar.

TIP

These cupcakes are perfect for Bonfire Night.
To bash the toffees, unwrap them and place them in a zip-lock freezer bag. Make sure you remove the excess air from the bag before sealing it, then bash the bag with a rolling pin until the toffees are broken up into small pieces.

COFFEE AND PECAN CUPCAKES

MAKES 12

For the cakes

125g (½ cup, plus 1 tbsp) unsalted butter, softened

125g (⅔ cup) soft light brown muscovado sugar

2 large eggs

125g (1 cup) self-raising flour

1 tsp baking powder

2 tsp instant espresso powder mixed with 2 tbsp boiling water (cooled)

50g (½ cup) chopped pecans

To decorate

150g (⅔ cup) unsalted butter, at room temperature

250g (1¾ cups) icing (powdered) sugar

2 tsp instant espresso powder mixed with 1 tbsp boiling water (cooled)

1-2 tbsp milk

chocolate coffee beans

edible gold sugar

Preheat the oven to 180°C/350°F/gas 4. Line a 12-hole muffin tin with paper cupcake cases.

To make the cakes, place the butter and sugar in a large bowl and beat with an electric whisk until pale and fluffy. Add the eggs, one at a time, beating well between each addition. Sift over the flour and baking powder and fold in with a large metal spoon. Pour in the cooled espresso, add the pecans and fold together. Divide the mixture evenly between the paper cases and smooth the tops with the back of a spoon.

Bake for 18 minutes, or until the sponge springs back when pressed with your finger. Remove the cakes from the tin and place on a wire rack to cool.

For the icing, beat together the butter and icing sugar with an electric whisk until pale and fluffy. Stir in the cooled espresso and enough milk to make a light, fluffy icing. Spoon the icing into a piping bag fitted with a star nozzle.

When the cakes are cool, pipe the icing onto each cake and top with chocolate coffee beans and a sprinkling of edible gold sugar.

LEMON AND ALMOND DRIZZLE CUPCAKES

MAKES 12

125g (½ cup, plus 1 tbsp) unsalted butter, softened

125g (⅔ cup, minus 2 tsp) golden caster (superfine) sugar

2 large eggs

75g (½ cup, plus ½ tbsp) self-raising flour

1½ tsp baking powder

50g (½ cup) ground almonds

2 unwaxed lemons

1–2 tbsp milk

40g (3 tbsp) demerara (turbinado) sugar

Preheat the oven to 180°C/350°F/gas 4. Line a 12-hole muffin tin with paper cupcake cases.

To make the cakes, place the butter and caster sugar in a large bowl and beat with an electric whisk until pale and fluffy. Add the eggs, one at a time, beating well between each addition. Sift over the flour and baking powder and fold in using a large metal spoon. Fold in the ground almonds, the finely grated zest of one lemon and enough milk for the mixture to be of a dropping consistency.

Divide the mixture evenly between the paper cases and smooth the tops with the back of a spoon. Bake for 18–20 minutes, or until well risen and slightly springy to the touch.

Meanwhile, mix together the juice of one lemon and half the zest of the remaining lemon with the demerara sugar to make a lemon syrup.

Remove the cakes from the oven and, while they are still hot, use a toothpick to poke little holes in the top of each one. Pour the lemon syrup over each cake and allow it to be absorbed before adding any more. Set aside for 10 minutes. Scatter with extra lemon zest before serving.

(pictured overleaf with flags)

CARROT, APPLE AND PECAN CUPCAKES

MAKES 12

For the cakes

100g (3½oz) carrots, finely grated

1 apple (about 125g/4½oz), peeled, cored and cut into small cubes

1 tsp ground cinnamon

1 orange, finely grated zest

100g (½ cup) soft brown sugar

pinch of salt

85ml (⅓ cup) mild olive oil

2 large eggs, beaten

125g (1 cup) self-raising flour

½ tsp baking powder

½ tsp bicarbonate of soda (baking soda)

To decorate

50g (3½ tbsp) unsalted butter, softened

150g (¾ cup) mascarpone cheese

3 tbsp maple syrup

1 orange, finely grated zest, and 2 tsp orange juice

12 pecan halves

Preheat the oven to 180°C/350°F/gas 4. Line a 12-hole cupcake tin with paper cupcake cases.

To make the cakes, place the grated carrots in a bowl with the apple, cinnamon, orange zest, sugar, salt, oil and eggs and whisk together until combined. Sift over the flour, baking powder and bicarbonate of soda and fold in until combined.

Divide the mixture evenly between the paper cases and smooth the tops with a spatula. Bake for 18 minutes, or until risen and springy to the touch. Remove from the oven and set aside for 5 minutes before placing on a wire rack to cool completely.

For the icing, beat together the butter and mascarpone until light and fluffy. Beat in the maple syrup, half the orange zest and the orange juice. Once the cakes are cool, place a spoonful of icing on top of each and smooth with a palette knife. Place a pecan half on top of each cake before serving.

(pictured overleaf)

STICKY GINGER CUPCAKES

MAKES 12

For the cakes

125g (1 cup) self-raising flour

1 tsp ground ginger

½ tsp bicarbonate of soda (baking soda)

pinch salt

85g (¼ cup) golden syrup (light corn syrup)

1 tbsp treacle (blackstrap molasses)

2 tbsp syrup from the ginger jar

60g (4 tbsp) soft dark brown sugar

60g (¼ cup) unsalted butter

1 piece stem ginger in syrup, chopped

40ml (2½ tbsp) milk

1 large egg

To decorate

150g (¾ cup) mascarpone cheese

75ml (⅓ cup) whipping cream

¼ tsp ground ginger

2 tbsp ginger syrup

1 stem ginger ball, finely sliced

Preheat the oven to 180°C/350°F/gas 4. Line a 12-hole muffin tin with paper cupcake cases.

Sift the flour, ground ginger and bicarbonate of soda into a large bowl and add the salt. Put the golden syrup, treacle, ginger syrup, sugar and butter into a medium saucepan. Place over a low heat, stirring until the butter and sugar have melted. Stir in the stem ginger, remove from the heat then pour into the dry ingredients and mix together using a large metal spoon.

In a jug, measure out the milk and whisk in the egg. Pour the milk mixture into the flour mixture and fold together until well combined (the mixture will be quite wet at this stage). Divide the mixture evenly between the paper cases.

Bake for 20 minutes, or until a skewer inserted into the cakes comes out clean. Leave to cool for 5 minutes in the tin, then transfer to a wire rack.

For the icing, beat the mascarpone and cream until smooth, then fold in the ground ginger and ginger syrup. Set aside. Place a spoonful of the icing on top of each of the cooled cakes and arrange the sliced stem ginger on top.

COCONUT, LEMON AND ELDERFLOWER CUPCAKES

MAKES 12

For the cakes

125g (½ cup, plus 1 tbsp) unsalted butter, softened

125g (⅔ cup, minus 2 tsp) golden caster (superfine) sugar

2 large eggs

75g (½ cup, plus ½ tbsp) self-raising flour

1½ tsp baking powder

50g (⅔ cup) desiccated coconut

1 lemon, finely grated zest

2–3 tbsp elderflower cordial

To decorate

150g (⅔ cup) unsalted butter, softened

250g (1¾ cups) icing (powdered) sugar

3 tbsp elderflower cordial

1 lemon, finely grated zest of ½ lemon, and 2 tsp juice

2 tbsp coconut flakes or desiccated coconut, toasted

Preheat the oven to 180°C/350°F/gas 4. Line a 12-hole muffin tin with paper cupcake cases.

To make the cakes, place the butter and sugar in a large bowl and beat with an electric whisk until pale and fluffy. Add the eggs, one at a time, beating well between each addition. Sift over the flour and baking powder and fold in using a large metal spoon. Add the desiccated coconut, lemon zest and enough elderflower cordial for the mixture to be of a dropping consistency.

Divide the mixture evenly between the paper cases and smooth the tops with the back of a spoon. Bake for 18 minutes, or until well risen and springy to the touch. Remove the cakes from the tin and place on a wire rack to cool.

For the icing, beat the butter and icing sugar together in a large bowl with an electric whisk until pale and fluffy. Add the elderflower cordial, half the lemon zest and the lemon juice, and beat until well combined. Spoon into a piping bag fitted with a star nozzle. When the cakes are cool, pipe the icing onto each cake and scatter with toasted coconut flakes and the remaining lemon zest before serving.

PISTACHIO AND POMEGRANATE CUPCAKES

MAKES 12

For the cakes

125g (½ cup, plus 1 tbsp) unsalted butter, softened

125g (⅔ cup, minus 2 tsp) golden caster (superfine) sugar

2 large eggs

100g (¾ cup) self-raising flour

1½ tsp baking powder

25g (¼ cup) nibbed or shelled pistachios, roughly chopped

½ orange, finely grated zest

1–2 tbsp pomegranate juice

To decorate

200g (1½ cups, minus 1 tbsp) icing (powdered) sugar

2–3 tbsp fresh pomegranate juice

15g (⅛ cup) nibbed or chopped pistachios

2 tbsp pomegranate seeds

Preheat the oven to 180°C/350°F/gas 4. Line a 12-hole muffin tin with paper cupcake cases.

To make the cakes, place the butter and sugar in a large bowl and beat with an electric whisk until pale and fluffy. Add the eggs, one at a time, beating well between each addition. Sift over the flour and baking powder and fold in using a large metal spoon. Add the pistachios, orange zest and enough pomegranate juice for the mixture to be of a dropping consistency.

Divide the mixture evenly between the paper cases and smooth the tops with the back of a spoon. Bake for 18 minutes, or until well risen and slightly springy to the touch. Remove the cakes from the tin and leave to cool on a wire rack.

For the icing, place the icing sugar in a large bowl and beat in enough pomegranate juice to make a pourable icing. Spoon over the top of each of the cooled cupcakes. Decorate with the pistachios and pomegranate seeds before serving.

LAVENDER CUPCAKES

MAKES 12

For the cakes

3 tbsp milk

1 tbsp dried culinary lavender flowers
(available online or from large supermarkets)

125g (½ cup plus 1 tbsp)
unsalted butter, softened

125g (⅔ cup minus 2 tsp) golden
caster (superfine) sugar

2 large eggs

125g (1 cup) self-raising flour

1 tsp baking powder

½ tsp vanilla extract

To decorate

200g (1½ cups minus 1 tbsp)
fondant icing sugar

½ tsp vanilla extract

a drop of purple gel food colouring

sugared flowers and rainbow dust

Preheat the oven to 180°C/350°F/gas 4. Line a 12-hole muffin tin with paper cupcake cases.

Pour the milk into a small pan, add the dried lavender flowers and place over a low heat for 1–2 minutes. Remove from the heat and set aside to cool.

For the cakes, place the butter and sugar in a large bowl and beat with an electric whisk until pale and fluffy. Add the eggs, one at a time, beating between each addition. Sift over the flour and baking powder and fold in using a metal spoon. Strain the lavender milk through a sieve into a bowl, pressing the flowers to extract the flavour, then discard the flowers. Stir 2 tbsp of the lavender-infused milk into the cake mix (reserve the rest for the icing), along with the vanilla extract.

Divide the mixture evenly between the paper cases and smooth the tops with the back of a spoon. Bake for 18 minutes, or until well risen and springy to the touch. Remove the cakes from the tin and transfer to a wire rack to cool.

For the icing, place the fondant icing sugar in bowl, add the reserved lavender milk, 1–2 tablespoons of cold water, the vanilla extract and the food colouring. Mix until you have a thick paste, which should drop, not run, off the spoon. If it's too runny, add more icing sugar. Spoon a teaspoon of icing onto each cooled cake. Scatter with sugared flowers and rainbow dust.

CHOCOLATE CAKES

CHOCOLATE CAKES

. . . .

We're all chocoholics, and our selection of celebratory chocolate recipes won't disappoint! Recipes include gooey chocolate brownies, individual triple chocolate cheesecakes, mini pavlovas and moreish salted caramel billionaire's shortcake. These cakes are all easy to assemble, indulgently decadent and above all, completely delicious.

There are certain ingredients that always work well together, and all the classics are here. We've combined dark, milk and white chocolate with cherries, nuts, fudge, salted caramel and even carrots. Perfect for a tea party, a dinner-party dessert or just as a decadent mid-afternoon treat, sometimes chocolate is the only answer!

SOUR CHERRY AND CHOCOLATE BROWNIES

MAKES 16–20 SQUARES

250g (1 cup, plus 2 tbsp) salted butter, softened, plus extra to grease

150g (¾ cup) golden caster (superfine) sugar

100g (½ cup) light brown muscovado sugar

200g (1¼ cups) good-quality dark (bitter-sweet) chocolate (70 per cent cocoa solids), broken into squares

3 large eggs, plus 1 extra egg yolk, beaten

60g (½ cup) plain (all-purpose) flour

60g (⅔ cup) finest-quality cocoa powder, plus extra for dusting

½ tsp baking powder

60g (scant ½ cup) dried sour cherries

75g (½ cup) white chocolate, roughly chopped

Preheat the oven to 180°C/350°F/gas 4. Lightly grease a 23cm (9in) square baking tin and line it with baking paper.

Put both types of sugar and the butter in a large bowl and beat with an electric whisk for several minutes until pale and fluffy.

Place the dark chocolate (reserving 30g/1oz for later) in a microwaveable bowl and melt in 30-second bursts in the microwave, stirring between each burst. Set aside and leave to cool slightly. Alternatively, place the chocolate in a small heatproof bowl that fits snugly over a pan of gently simmering water and leave for a few minutes to melt.

Add the eggs to the butter mixture gradually, beating well between each addition. Fold in the melted chocolate. Chop the remaining dark chocolate into small chunks and fold into the mixture. Lastly, sift over the flour, cocoa powder and baking powder, and gently but firmly fold in with the sour cherries without knocking any of the air out. Stir in the white chocolate.

Recipe continues overleaf

Scrape the mixture into the prepared tin, smooth the top and bake for 25–28 minutes, checking after 25 minutes. When it is cooked, the top will have risen slightly and the brownie will appear slightly softer in the middle than around the edges. If it is not ready, cook for a further 3 minutes, then remove from the oven.

Leave to cool for 5 minutes in the tin, then transfer (with the baking paper) to a wire rack to cool. Don't leave the brownie to cool completely in the tin or it will carry on cooking and will no longer be gooey in the middle. It will solidify a little on cooling, so if it appears a bit wet, don't worry; it will be perfect.

Turn out onto a board, leave to cool slightly, then peel off the baking paper. Dust with cocoa powder and cut into squares before serving.

VARIATION

You can also add 50g (1¾oz) chopped pecans or walnuts to these brownies, if you like. These should be gooey in the middle with nuggets of molten chocolate and sour cherries to cut through the richness.

TRIPLE CHOCOLATE CHEESECAKES

MAKES 8

For the bottom layer
150g (1¼ cups) chocolate ginger biscuits
60g (¼ cup) unsalted butter, melted
¼ tsp ground ginger

For the middle layer
150g (1 cup) good-quality dark (bitter-sweet) chocolate (70 per cent cocoa solids), broken into squares
300g (1⅓ cups) soft cream cheese, at room temperature
200ml (¾ cup) double (heavy) or whipping cream

75g (½ cup plus ½ tbsp) icing (powdered) sugar
1 piece stem ginger, finely chopped
3 tbsp syrup from the ginger jar

For the top layer
275ml (1 cup) double (heavy) cream
100g (⅔ cup) white chocolate, broken into squares
100g (1¼ cups) white and dark chocolate curls
chocolate stars
edible silver glitter

For the bottom layer, blitz the ginger biscuits in a blender until they turn to crumbs. Add the melted butter and ground ginger and blitz until combined Divide the mixture between eight straight-sided glasses and press down gently to form an even layer. Chill while you prepare the middle layer.

Place the chocolate in a microwavable bowl and melt in 30-second bursts in the microwave, stirring between each burst. Set aside. Beat the cream cheese with an electric whisk until softened, add the melted chocolate, cream, icing sugar, stem ginger and syrup and beat until smooth. Spoon into a piping bag fitted with a straight nozzle, pipe in an even layer on top of the bottom layer and chill again.

For the top layer, whip the cream until it forms soft peaks. Place the white chocolate in a microwavable bowl and melt in 30-second bursts in the microwave, stirring between each burst. Fold the melted chocolate into the whipped cream. Spoon into a piping bag fitted with a star nozzle, pipe on top of the middle layer and chill until needed. Decorate with white and dark chocolate curls, chocolate stars and edible silver glitter before serving.

DOUBLE CHOCOLATE FUDGE CUPCAKES

MAKES 12

For the cakes	*To decorate*
25g (⅛ cup) good-quality dark (bitter-sweet) chocolate (70 per cent cocoa solids), broken into squares	100g (⅔ cup) good-quality dark (bitter-sweet) chocolate (70 per cent cocoa solids), broken into squares
25g (2 tbsp) cocoa powder	150g (⅔ cup) unsalted butter
100g (¾ cup) self-raising flour	200g (1½ cups, minus 1 tbsp) icing (powdered) sugar
1 tsp baking powder	
125g (½ cup, plus 1 tbsp) salted butter, at room temperature	3 tbsp cocoa powder
	2 tsp vanilla extract
125g (⅔ cup) light muscovado sugar	2 tbsp milk
2 large eggs	gold or silver edible glitter
2–3 tbsp milk	gold or silver stars
50g (⅓ cup) white chocolate, roughly chopped	red sugar roses

Preheat the oven to 180°C/350°F/gas 4. Line a 12-hole muffin tin with paper cupcake cases.

To make the cakes, place the dark chocolate in a small microwavable bowl and melt in 30-second bursts in the microwave, stirring between each burst, then set aside. Alternatively, place the chocolate in a small heatproof bowl that fits snugly over a pan of gently simmering water and leave for a few minutes to melt. Set aside to cool while you prepare the rest of the ingredients.

Recipe continues overleaf

Sift the cocoa powder, flour and baking powder into a bowl.

Place the butter and sugar in a separate large bowl and beat with an electric whisk for about 5 minutes until pale and fluffy. Add the eggs, one at a time, beating well between each addition. Then, using a large metal spoon, fold in half the dry ingredients followed by the melted chocolate. Fold in the rest of the dry ingredients, followed by enough milk for the mixture to be of a dropping consistency. Finally, fold in the white chocolate.

Divide the mixture evenly between the paper cases and smooth the tops with a spatula. Bake for 18 minutes, or until slightly springy to the touch. Remove the cakes from the tin and leave to cool on a wire rack.

For the fudge icing, place the chocolate in a small microwavable bowl and melt in 30-second bursts in the microwave, stirring between each burst, then set aside. Alternatively, place the chocolate in a small heatproof bowl that fits snugly over a pan of gently simmering water and leave for a few minutes to melt. Beat the butter, icing sugar and cocoa powder together with an electric whisk until fluffy. This will take about 5 minutes. Add the vanilla extract and melted chocolate, and beat until combined and smooth. Finally, beat in the milk to make a light, fluffy icing.

Spoon the icing into a piping bag fitted with a star nozzle and pipe icing onto the top of each cake. Sprinkle with gold or silver edible glitter and stars or sugar roses before serving.

CHOCOLATE AND CHERRY PAVLOVAS

MAKES 8

3 large egg whites

150g (¾ cup) golden caster (superfine) sugar

1 tsp cornflour (cornstarch)

½ tsp balsamic vinegar

2 tsp cocoa powder

400ml (1¾ cups) double (heavy) cream

100g (3½oz) tinned black cherries in syrup, drained, or fresh cherries

2 tbsp syrup from the black cherries

2 tbsp icing (powdered) sugar

chocolate curls

edible gold dust

Preheat the oven to 140°C/275°F/gas 1. Line a large baking sheet with baking paper.

In a large, clean bowl, whisk the egg whites with an electric whisk until stiff – you should be able to turn the bowl upside down without the eggs falling out. Gradually add the golden caster sugar to the egg whites, beating hard until all the sugar is incorporated and the mixture is stiff and glossy.

Whisk in the cornflour and vinegar, then fold in the cocoa powder, but not too thoroughly as you want a chocolate ripple effect.

Spoon the meringue into eight even circles on the baking sheet, spacing them well apart. Use a spatula to peak the sides up slightly so that they are higher than the middle.

Bake for 45–50 minutes, or until firm to the touch. Turn off the oven and leave the meringues to cool in the oven for 1 hour.

Meanwhile, whip the cream, syrup and icing sugar together until the mixture forms soft peaks.

Once the meringues are totally cool, spoon a little cream into the middle of each, place three tinned cherries or fresh cherries on top and sprinkle with chocolate curls and gold dust before serving.

NUTTY CHOCOLATE CARROT CAKE

MAKES 16 SQUARES

For the cake
unsalted butter, for greasing
175g (1⅓ cups) plain (all-purpose) flour
1 tsp baking powder
1 tsp bicarbonate of soda (baking soda)
¼ tsp fine sea salt
300ml (1¼ cups) light olive or sunflower oil
100g (½ cup) soft dark brown sugar
200g (1 cup) light muscovado sugar
3 large eggs

225g raw carrots, peeled and grated
75g (½ cup) hazelnuts, lightly toasted, and roughly chopped

For the icing
125g (4½oz) chocolate hazelnut spread
60g (½ cup) icing (powdered) sugar
1 tbsp cocoa powder
100ml (scant ½ cup) double (heavy) cream

Preheat the oven to 180°C/350°F/gas 4. Lightly grease a 20cm (8in) square non-stick baking tin and line it with baking paper so that the paper hangs over the edges by 2cm (¾in).

To make the cake, sift the flour, baking powder and bicarbonate of soda into a small bowl. Add the salt and set aside. Pour the oil into a separate large bowl, add the two types of sugar and beat until well combined. Add the eggs, one at a time, beating well between each addition. Fold in the flour mixture, carrots and 50g (⅓ cup) of the hazelnuts (reserving the rest for later). Spoon the mixture into the prepared tin and smooth the surface flat.

Bake on the middle shelf for 45 minutes. Turn the oven down to 170°C/325°F/gas 3 and bake for 20–25 minutes, or until a skewer inserted into the middle of the cake comes out clean. Leave to cool for 10 minutes, then remove the cake from the tin and cool on a wire rack.

For the icing, place the chocolate hazelnut spread in a bowl with the icing sugar, cocoa powder and cream. Beat with an electric whisk until combined and fluffy. When the cake is completely cool, spread the icing over the top and scatter with the remaining hazelnuts. Cut into squares and serve.

BLACK FOREST GÂTEAU CUPCAKES

MAKES 12

For the cakes

50g (2 oz) good-quality dark (bitter-sweet) chocolate (70 per cent cocoa solids), broken into squares

125g (½ cup, plus 1 tbsp) unsalted butter, softened

100g (½ cup) caster (superfine) sugar

25g (2 tbsp) light brown muscovado sugar

2 large eggs

100g (¾ cup) self-raising flour

25g (2 tbsp) cocoa powder

1 tsp baking powder

2 tbsp milk

To decorate

4 tbsp good-quality black cherry jam

300ml (1¼ cups) double (heavy) cream

1 tsp vanilla extract

3 tbsp icing (powdered) sugar

12 fresh cherries with stalks

chocolate curls

edible gold stars and glitter

Preheat the oven to 180°C/350°F/gas 4. Line a 12-hole muffin tin with paper cupcake cases.

To make the cakes, place the chocolate in a small microwaveable bowl and melt in 30-second bursts in the microwave, stirring between each burst, then set aside. Alternatively, place the chocolate in a small heatproof bowl that fits snugly over a pan of gently simmering water and leave for a few minutes to melt.

In a separate bowl, beat together the butter and both sugars until pale and fluffy. Add the eggs, one at a time, beating well between each addition. Sift over the flour, cocoa powder and baking powder, and fold in with a large metal spoon. Add the milk and finally fold in the melted chocolate.

Recipe continues overleaf

Divide the mixture evenly between the paper cases and smooth the tops with the back of a spoon.

Bake for 18 minutes, or until a skewer inserted into the middle of each cake comes out clean. Remove the cakes from the tin and leave to cool on a wire rack.

Once cool, scoop out a teaspoonful of mixture from the top of each cake and spoon in a teaspoonful of jam.

Whip the cream, vanilla extract and icing sugar together until the mixture forms soft peaks. Pipe some cream onto each cake and top with a cherry, chocolate curls, gold stars and glitter.

VARIATION

If you would like to make these in advance, prepare the cakes, leave to cool completely, then store in an airtight container for up to 2 days. When you are ready to serve, finish with the jam and cream topping. They are best eaten the day they are made (if you want to make them with the topping).

SALTED CARAMEL BILLIONAIRE'S SHORTCAKE

MAKES 16–20 SQUARES

For the bottom layer

300g (2½ cups) digestive biscuits

125g (½ cup, plus 1 tbsp) salted butter, melted

For the caramel layer

100g (½ cup, minus 1 tbsp) salted butter, plus extra for greasing

1 x 397g (14oz) can condensed milk

75g (6 tbsp) light muscovado sugar

75g (¼ cup) golden syrup

1 vanilla pod (bean), seeds scraped

a pinch of sea salt

For the top layer

150g (5½oz) good-quality dark (bitter-sweet) chocolate (70 per cent cocoa solids), broken into squares

50g (2oz) white chocolate, broken into squares

edible gold or silver stars

Lightly grease a 20cm (8in) square baking tray and line it with baking paper.

To make the bottom layer, place the digestives in a blender and blitz until they form crumbs. Pour in the melted butter and blitz until combined.

Tip the biscuit mixture into the prepared tin and press down with a potato masher or flat-bottomed glass to make an even layer. Place in the fridge and chill while you prepare the caramel.

Pour all the caramel ingredients into a saucepan, place over a low heat and stir constantly until melted. Keep a close eye on the mixture, keeping the heat low, and stir continuously as it can catch on the bottom of the pan. Bring to a simmer and bubble for 10 minutes, or until the mixture starts to thicken and deepens to a darker caramel colour. Discard the vanilla pod.

Recipe continues overleaf

Pour the caramel over the biscuit base and leave to chill for at least 2 hours, until set.

For the top layer, place the dark chocolate in a microwavable bowl and melt in 30-second bursts in the microwave, stirring between each burst. Repeat with the white chocolate in a separate bowl.

Pour the dark chocolate over the whole of the cake, then place dollops of the white chocolate on top. Then, using a toothpick, swirl the top to create a marbled effect. Sprinkle with gold or silver stars, cover and chill in the fridge for 1 hour, or until totally set.

Cut into squares to serve.

TIP

These are a simplified version of millionaire's shortbread, and don't require you to bake biscuits for the bottom. They taste just as yummy and they take half the time to make! Sprinkle with gold or silver stars to make them worthy of a billionaire!

CHOCOLATE BISCUIT CAKE

MAKES 16 PIECES

100g (½ cup, minus 1 tbsp) unsalted butter, cut into cubes, plus extra for greasing

200g (1¼ cups) good-quality dark (bitter-sweet) chocolate (70 per cent cocoa solids), broken into squares

100g (⅔ cup) milk chocolate, broken into squares

100g (¼ cup, plus 1 tbsp) golden syrup

250g (2 cups) digestive biscuits

50g (⅓ cup) sultanas (golden raisins)

40g (¼ cup) dried apricots, chopped

50g (⅓ cup) sour dried cherries (optional)

Lightly grease a 20cm (8in) square tin and line it with cling film (plastic wrap) with 2cm (¾in) hanging over the edges. This is essential so that you can remove the biscuit cake from the tin once it has chilled.

Put the butter, both types of chocolate and golden syrup in a heatproof bowl that fits snugly over a pan of gently simmering water. Stir until melted.

Meanwhile, place the digestives in a zip-lock bag and bash with a rolling pin until they are coarsely broken with some bigger bits.

Remove the chocolate mixture from the heat, add the bashed digestives, sultanas, apricots and dried cherries (if using) and stir together.

Spoon the biscuit mixture into the prepared tin and smooth the surface flat. Place in the fridge and chill for at least 1 hour.

Carefully lift out the biscuit cake, remove the cling film and cut into triangle-shaped pieces.

(pictured left overleaf)

CHOCOLATE CRISPY CAKES

MAKES 24

75g (½ cup) milk chocolate, broken into squares

75g (½ cup) good-quality dark (bitter-sweet) chocolate (70 per cent cocoa solids), broken into squares

100g (¼ cup, plus 1 tbsp) golden syrup (light corn syrup)

75g (⅓ cup) unsalted butter

50g (⅓ cup) sultanas (golden raisins) (optional)

100g (4 cups) corn flakes

coloured sugar-coated chocolate buttons, to decorate

Line a 24-hole mini cupcake tin with paper cupcake cases.

Place both types of chocolate, the golden syrup and butter in a bowl that fits snugly over a pan of gently simmering water, and stir until melted and combined.

Remove from the heat and leave to cool for a few minutes (otherwise the cornflakes will go soft).

Add the sultanas (if using) and corn flakes, and stir well with a wooden spoon to coat all the corn flakes in chocolate.

Divide the mixture evenly between the paper cases. Decorate with chocolate buttons and chill for at least 1 hour before serving.

(pictured right overleaf)

ALMOND AND CHOCOLATE MACAROONS

MAKES 30

200g (1⅓ cups) blanched almonds

2 large egg whites

225g (1 cup, plus ½ tbsp) golden caster (superfine) sugar

30g (¼ cup) cornflour (cornstarch), sifted

1 tsp almond extract

200g (1¼ cups) good-quality dark (bitter-sweet) chocolate (70 per cent cocoa solids), chopped and melted (optional)

100g (⅔ cup) white chocolate, chopped and melted (optional)

Preheat the oven to 180°C/350°F/gas 4. Line two baking sheets with baking paper.

Place the almonds on a baking tray and toast them at the top of the oven for 5 minutes, or until golden brown, then set aside to cool.

In a large bowl, whisk the egg whites until stiff peaks form. Add the sugar a little at a time, whisking between each addition, until all the sugar is incorporated and the mixture is thick and glossy.

In a food processor, blitz the cooled almonds to a coarse powder (reserving 30 almonds for decorating). Fold the almonds and cornflour into the meringue mixture. Fold in the almond extract. Cover and chill for 30 minutes.

Place teaspoons of the mixture onto the prepared baking sheets, spacing them at least 4cm (1½in) apart as they will spread. Try to keep the mixture in small, round heaps. Place a whole almond in the middle of each heap.

Bake at the top of the oven for 12 minutes, or until the exterior is crisp and the edges start to colour slightly. Leave the macaroons to cool on their trays for 5 minutes, then transfer to a wire rack to cool completely.

If liked, dip the flat base of the biscuits in the melted dark chocolate and leave to set, flat-side up, on the wire rack. Drizzle the dark chocolate with a little melted white chocolate. Dip a few of the bases in white chocolate, and drizzle with dark chocolate. Leave to set completely before serving.

CHOCOLATE BERRY MARBLE CUPCAKES

MAKES 12

For the cakes

125g (½ cup, plus 1 tbsp) unsalted butter, softened

125g (⅔ cup minus 2 tsp) golden caster (superfine) sugar

2 large eggs

125g (1 cup) self-raising flour

1 tsp baking powder

1 tsp vanilla extract

1–2 tbsp milk

100g (¾ cup) raspberries

30g (⅛ cup) white chocolate, chopped

For the white chocolate icing

100g (⅔ cup) white chocolate

140g (⅔ cup) unsalted butter, softened

140g (1 cup) icing (powdered) sugar

For the dark chocolate icing

100g (⅔ cup) good-quality dark (bitter-sweet) chocolate (70 per cent cocoa solids)

150g (⅔ cup) unsalted butter, softened

200g (1½ cups minus 1 tbsp) icing (powdered) sugar

3 tbsp cocoa powder

2–3 tbsp milk

2 tsp vanilla extract

chocolate hearts, edible glitter and 12 fresh raspberries, to decorate

Preheat the oven to 180°C/350°F/gas 4. Line a 12-hole muffin tin with paper cupcake cases.

To make the cakes, beat the butter and sugar with an electric whisk until pale and fluffy. Add the eggs, one at a time, beating between each addition. Sift over the flour and baking powder. Fold in using a metal spoon. Add the vanilla extract and enough milk for the mixture to be of a dropping consistency. Spoon half into a separate bowl and add the raspberries. Mash so the mixture is streaked pink, then set aside. Stir the white chocolate into the non-raspberry mixture.

Recipe continues overleaf

Place alternate dollops of the white chocolate and raspberry mixtures into the cupcake cases until the mixtures are evenly distributed. Smooth the tops with the back of a spoon and bake for 18 minutes, or until well risen and springy to the touch. Remove from the tin and transfer to a wire rack to cool.

Meanwhile, make the icings. For the white chocolate icing, melt the chocolate, broken into squares, in 30-second bursts in the microwave, stirring between each burst, then set aside. Beat the butter and icing sugar with an electric whisk until pale and fluffy, then beat in the melted chocolate until smooth.

For the dark chocolate icing, melt the chocolate, broken into squares, in 30-second bursts in the microwave, stirring between each burst, then set aside. Beat the butter, icing sugar and cocoa powder in a large bowl with an electric whisk until pale and fluffy, then fold in the melted chocolate, milk and vanilla extract.

Spoon the white chocolate icing down one side of an piping bag fitted with a star nozzle and spoon the dark chocolate icing down the other side.

Once the cupcakes are cool, pipe the icing onto the top of each cake, creating a marbled effect, and decorate with chocolate hearts and glitter. Top each one with a raspberry.

KIDS'
CAKES

KIDS' CAKES

....

Children love cake, from bright and colourful birthday cakes to
little fairy cakes, so we couldn't resist letting our imaginations run
wild when creating these playful bakes. Our quick and easy recipes
are the perfect way to get budding bakers started in the kitchen.

With fun, eye-catching recipes for flower cakes, snakes and ladders
cupcakes and fudge nests topped with marshmallows and sweeties,
jelly snakes and toffee ladders or fluffy chicks, there's plenty of
baking inspiration to keep your little ones occupied on rainy days.
For big kids there are nostalgic lemon fairy cakes and cupcakes
baked in waffle cones, resembling traditional ice cream cones.

We've also included ideas for larger cakes that will make stunning
centrepieces for birthday parties and celebrations. There's a train
laden with sweeties, a pretty butterfly and an amazing multi-
coloured rainbow cake – whatever you choose, you are sure to
put a smile on the birthday girl or boy's face. Just add
candles – and don't forget to make a birthday wish!

SNAKES AND LADDERS PARTY CUPCAKES

MAKES 12

For the cakes

125g (½ cup, plus 1 tbsp) unsalted butter, softened

125g (⅔ cup, minus 2 tsp) golden caster (superfine) sugar

2 large eggs

125g (1 cup) self-raising flour

1 tsp baking powder

1 orange, finely grated zest

2 tbsp orange juice

To decorate

200g (1½ cups, minus 1 tbsp) fondant icing sugar

1 tsp orange or vanilla extract

pink and blue gel food colourings

black or brown writing icing pen

4 jelly snakes

2 chocolate-covered toffee bars, cut in half horizontally to make 4 ladders

Preheat the oven to 180°C/350°F/gas 4. Line a 12-hole muffin tin with paper cupcake cases.

To make the cakes, place the butter and sugar in a large bowl and beat with an electric whisk until pale and fluffy. Add the eggs, one at a time, beating well between each addition. Sift over the flour and baking powder and fold in using a large metal spoon. Add the orange zest and juice to make a dropping consistency.

Divide the mixture evenly between the paper cases and smooth the tops with the back of a spoon. Bake for 18 minutes, or until well risen and slightly springy to the touch. Remove the cakes from the oven and transfer to a wire rack to cool.

For the icing, put the fondant icing sugar in a large bowl, add the orange extract and 2 tsp of cold water to make a thick, spoonable icing. Add a little

Recipe continues overleaf

more water if the mixture is too thick. Spoon half the icing into a separate bowl, add a little pink colouring to it and stir until it is your desired colour. Add a little blue colouring to the other bowl and mix well.

When the cupcakes are cool, spoon the pink icing over half the cakes and the blue icing over the other half. Leave to set for 1 hour.

Arrange the cupcakes into a grid on a square board. Use the writing icing pen to write the numbers 1 to 12 on each cupcake. Then place the jelly snakes and chocolate ladders on the top to create the snakes and ladders game and serve.

TIP

If you want to make a larger game, you can easily
double the quantities to make 24 cupcakes.
Alternatively, you could make 24 mini cupcakes – just
divide the mixture between 24 mini cupcake cases
and bake for about 12 minutes, or until springy to the
touch and a skewer inserted into the middle of the
cakes comes out clean.

TRAIN CAKE

SERVES 12

For the cake

225g (1 cup) unsalted butter, softened, plus extra for greasing

225g (1 cup, plus ½ tbsp) golden caster (superfine) sugar

4 large eggs

225g (1¾ cups) self-raising flour

40g (½ cup) cocoa powder

2 tsp baking powder

2 tsp vanilla extract

5–6 tbsp milk

For the buttercream

150g (⅔ cup) unsalted butter

235g (⅔ cup) icing (powdered) sugar

1 tbsp cocoa powder

1 tsp vanilla extract

1–2 tbsp milk

For the decorate

icing (powdered) sugar, for dusting

350g (12¼ oz) green ready-to-roll fondant icing

20 chocolate fingers

1 small chocolate Swiss roll

250g (6 oz) each of red, blue, yellow and orange ready-to-roll fondant icing

16 mini chocolate cookies with white cream filling

20 coloured sugar-coated chocolate buttons

2 chocolate cookies with white cream filling

1 bag coloured sugar-coated round sweets

30g (½ cup) mini marshmallows

1 small bag jelly beans

1 marshmallow

sugared flowers

Preheat the oven to 180°C/350°F/gas 4. Lightly grease a 20cm (8in) square non-stick deep baking tin with butter and line it with baking paper.

Start by making the cake. Place the butter and sugar in a large bowl and beat with an electric whisk until pale and fluffy. Add the eggs, one at a time, beating well between each addition. Sift over the flour, cocoa powder and

Recipe continues overleaf

baking powder and fold in using a large metal spoon. Add the vanilla extract and enough milk for the mixture to be of a dropping consistency. If the mixture looks like it is splitting, add a spoonful of the flour mixture before adding the next egg; this should help stabilize the mixture.

Spoon the mixture into the prepared tin and smooth the top with a spatula. Bake for 40 minutes, or until well risen and springy to the touch and when a skewer inserted into the middle comes out clean. If it isn't clean, bake for a further 5–10 minutes. Remove from the oven, peel off the baking paper and transfer to a wire rack to cool. Trim the edges with a serrated bread knife.

To make the buttercream, beat the butter, icing sugar, cocoa powder, vanilla extract and milk in a large bowl with an electric whisk until pale and fluffy.

Now make the decorations. Dust the work surface with icing sugar and roll out the green fondant icing to 5mm (¼in) thick. Brush a square 35 x 35cm (14 x 14in) cake board with a little buttercream to help the fondant icing stick, then cover with the fondant icing. Trim the edges with a sharp knife and cover with a line of chocolate fingers in a curve to make a train track.

Cut the cake into four 8 x 9cm (3¼ x 3½in) blocks for the carriages and the back of the engine. Cut them in half horizontally, spread with buttercream, then sandwich back together.

Cut a 9cm (3½in) piece of Swiss roll and attach it. with buttercream, to one of the rectangles, stood on its end, to make the engine. Spread with an even layer of buttercream. Roll out the red fondant icing on a clean surface lightly dusted with icing sugar and cover the engine with it. Roll out two 10cm (4in) thin sausage shapes of blue icing, brush with water (to help them stick) and press onto the front and back sides of the engine. Spread a dab of buttercream on four of the mini chocolate cookies and place a coloured sugar-coated chocolate button in the middle of each. Brush with buttercream and press onto the sides of the engine for wheels. Repeat with the larger chocolate cookies and place these on either side of the back of the engine. Add the large marshmallow to the front of the engine.

To make the first carriage, roll out the yellow fondant icing to 5mm (¼in) thick. Spread the outside of the carriage with buttercream and cover with the fondant icing. Roll out a 10cm (4in) thin sausage of red icing and use it to decorate the top of the rectangle. Attach it with a dab of water. Brush four small chocolate cookies with buttercream, press a coloured sugar-coated chocolate button into the middle of each and attach to the side of the carriage with buttercream. Fill the top with coloured sugar-coated sweets.

Repeat with the remaining two carriages, using orange and blue fondant icing. Decorate the tops with a thin sausage of a different-coloured fondant icing secured with water. Fill the carriages with mini marshmallows and jelly beans, or whichever sweets you prefer.

Place the engine at the front of the train track, then position the carriages behind it. Decorate around the train with sugared flowers and serve.

TIP

Ideally, make the cake a day in advance as it will be easier to ice. Alternatively, place the cooked cake in the freezer for 30 minutes so that less crumb will come off when you are icing it. Once iced, this cake will keep for 2–3 days, so it is a good one if you need to make a birthday cake in advance. Kids will love it!

LEMON BUTTERFLY FAIRY CAKES

MAKES 12

For the cakes

100g (½ cup, minus 1 tbsp) unsalted butter, softened

100g (½ cup) golden caster (superfine) sugar

2 large eggs

100g (¾ cup) self-raising flour

1 tsp baking powder

1 lemon, zest finely grated plus 2 tsp juice

1 tbsp milk

4 tbsp lemon curd

To decorate

75g (⅓ cup) unsalted butter, softened

150g (1 cup) icing (powdered) sugar, sifted, plus extra to dust

2–3 tsp lemon juice

lemon zest, to decorate

Preheat the oven to 180°C/350°F/gas 4. Line a 12-hole cupcake tin with paper fairy cake cases.

For the cakes, place the butter and sugar in a bowl and beat with an electric whisk until pale and fluffy. Add the eggs, one at a time, beating well between each addition. Sift over the flour and baking powder and fold in using a metal spoon. Add the lemon zest and juice and the milk and stir together until the mixture is of a dropping consistency. Add more milk as needed.

Divide the mixture evenly between the paper cases and smooth the tops with the back of a spoon. Bake for 16–18 minutes, or until well risen and slightly springy to the touch. Remove the cakes from the oven and transfer to a wire rack to cool.

Meanwhile, make the icing. Beat the butter and icing sugar in a large bowl with an electric whisk until pale and fluffy. Fold in 2 tsp of the lemon juice and beat until smooth. Spoon into a piping bag fitted with a star nozzle.

Once cool, cut a slice from the top of each cake and cut this slice in half. Place a teaspoon of lemon curd on top of each cake, pipe a small swirl of icing on top, then top with the half slices of cake to resemble butterfly wings. Dust the cakes with icing sugar and decorate with lemon zest to finish.

ICE CREAM CUPCAKES

MAKES 12

For the cakes

12 flat-bottomed waffle ice-cream cones

125g (½ cup, plus 1 tbsp) unsalted butter, softened

125g (⅔ cup, minus 2 tsp) caster (superfine) sugar

2 large eggs

125g (1 cup, minus 1 tbsp) self-raising flour

1 tsp baking powder

1 tsp vanilla extract

2 tbsp milk

To decorate

150g (⅔ cup) unsalted butter, softened

250g (1¾ cups) icing (powdered) sugar, sifted

2 tsp vanilla extract

6 chocolate flakes, cut in half

multi-coloured sprinkles

Preheat the oven to 180°C/350°F/gas 4. Line a 12-hole muffin tin with the flat-bottomed ice-cream cones.

To make the cakes, place the butter and sugar in a large bowl and beat with an electric whisk until pale and fluffy. Add the eggs, one at a time, beating well between each addition. Sift over the flour and baking powder and fold in with a large metal spoon. Finally, fold in the vanilla extract and milk.

Spoon the mixture into a piping bag fitted with a straight-ended nozzle and pipe the mixture into the ice-cream cones so that they are two-thirds full. Smooth the tops with the back of a spoon.

Bake for 25–30 minutes, or until a skewer inserted into the middle of each cake comes out clean. Remove the cakes from the tin and leave to cool on a wire rack.

For the icing, beat the butter, icing sugar and vanilla extract with an electric whisk until pale and fluffy. Spoon the icing into a piping bag fitted with a star nozzle and pipe icing onto the top of each cake in a swirl. Insert half a chocolate flake into the top of each and scatter with sprinkles.

FLOWER CAKES

For the cakes

125g (½ cup, plus 1 tbsp) unsalted butter, softened

125g (⅔ cup, minus 2 tsp) golden caster (superfine) sugar

2 large eggs

125g (1 cup) self-raising flour

1 tsp baking powder

1 tsp vanilla extract

2 tbsp milk

To decorate

250g (1¾ cups) icing (powdered) sugar

150g (⅔ cup) unsalted butter, softened

a few drops of green gel food colouring

1 tsp vanilla extract

12 marshmallows

80g (3oz) of coloured sugar-coated chocolate buttons

4 thin green straws, cut into 5cm (2in) lengths

Preheat the oven to 180°C/350°F/gas 4. Line a 12-hole muffin tin with paper cupcake cases.

To make the cakes, place the butter and sugar in a large bowl and beat with an electric whisk until pale and fluffy. Add the eggs, one at a time, beating well between each addition. Sift over the flour and baking powder and fold in using a metal spoon. Add the vanilla extract and milk and stir together.

Divide the mixture even between the paper cases and smooth with the back of a spoon. Bake for 18 minutes, or until well risen and slightly springy to the touch. Remove the cakes from the oven and transfer to a wire rack to cool.

To make the icing, place the icing sugar in a bowl with the butter and beat with an electric whisk until pale and fluffy. Add the food colouring and the vanilla extract, then beat together until well mixed. Spoon into a piping bag fitted with a star nozzle. Once cool, pipe the icing onto the top of the cakes.

Cut the face off the marshmallows so that you have a sticky circle, then stick on chocolate buttons in a flower shape. Stick straws into the marshmallows, insert the "flowers" into the top of the cakes and serve.

(pictured left overleaf)

STICKY TOFFEE MARSHMALLOW NESTS

MAKES 24 MINI NESTS

75g (2¾oz) marshmallows
75g (2¾oz) soft toffees
100g (½ cup minus 1 tbsp) unsalted butter, plus extra for greasing

100g (4 cups) puffed rice cereal
mini chocolate eggs and baby chicks, to decorate

Lightly grease a 24-hole mini cupcake tin.

Place the marshmallows, toffees and butter in a large heatproof bowl that fits snugly over a pan of gently simmering water and leave to melt, stirring occasionally.

When melted, remove from the heat and leave to cool for 2 minutes. Tip in the puffed rice cereal and stir to coat in the marshmallow mixture.

Using a lightly greased spoon, take spoonfuls of the mixture and press them into the prepared tin, pressing in the middle with your finger to make nest shapes.

Chill in the fridge for 30 minutes, then decorate with mini chocolate eggs and baby chicks.

(pictured right overleaf)

CHOCOLATE CHIP COOKIE ICE CREAM SANDWICHES

MAKES 6

125g (½ cup, plus 1 tbsp) salted butter, softened

75g (⅓ cup) granulated sugar

75g (6 tbsp) soft light brown muscovado sugar

1 large egg

240g (1¾ cups, plus 1 tbsp) plain (all-purpose) flour

¼ tsp salt

½ tsp bicarbonate of soda (baking soda)

75g (½ cup) dark chocolate chips

50g (⅓ cup) milk chocolate chips

50g (⅓ cup) white chocolate chips

vanilla ice cream, to serve

chocolate sprinkles

Line a baking sheet with baking paper.

Place the butter and both sugars in a large bowl and beat with an electric whisk until pale and fluffy. Beat in the egg, flour, salt and bicarbonate of soda, and finally stir in the chocolate chips.

Shape into 12 walnut-sized balls. Press down slightly and place spaced well apart on the prepared baking sheet. Cover and chill overnight in the fridge.

Preheat the oven to 180°C/350°F/gas 4. Bake straight from the fridge for 10–12 minutes, or until just turning golden but still slightly soft to touch. The cookies will continue to cook after coming out of the oven, so don't be tempted to bake them for longer or they will end up hard. Leave the cookies on the baking sheet for 2 minutes, then transfer to a wire rack to cool completely.

Once cool, place a dollop of ice cream between two cookies, sandwich together, dip the edge of the ice cream in chocolate sprinkles and eat immediately.

JAFFA CAKES

MAKES 12

For the cakes

unsalted butter, for greasing

50g (⅓ cup) plain (all-purpose) flour, plus extra for dusting

2 medium eggs

50g (¼ cup) golden caster (superfine) sugar

½ orange, finely grated zest

½ tsp orange extract

For the tops

135g (4¾oz) orange jelly

½ unwaxed orange, finely grated zest

1½ tbsp thin-cut marmalade

100g (3½oz) orange-flavoured dark chocolate (or add ½ tsp orange extract to the chocolate while it melts)

Preheat the oven to 180°C/350°F/gas 4. Lightly grease a 12-hole tart tin, dust it with plain flour, then shake out the excess.

To make the cakes, place the eggs and sugar in a heatproof bowl that fits snugly over a pan of gently simmering water. Beat continuously with an electric whisk until the mixture is pale and fluffy and has doubled in size. Sift over the flour and orange zest and fold in with a metal spoon. Fold in the orange extract. Don't over mix – you will knock out all the air and the bases will not be light and fluffy.

Divide the mixture between the holes of the tin. Bake for 8–10 minutes until risen and springy to the touch. Remove from the oven. Cool on a wire rack.

Cut the jelly into cubes, add 125ml (½ cup) boiling water, the orange zest and 2 tsp of marmalade (reserve the rest for later). Stir until melted. Grease and line a 15 x 25cm (5 x 10in) baking tray with cling film (plastic wrap), pour in the jelly so that it is 5mm (¼in) thick, then chill for 20 minutes, or until set. Once set, use a 4cm (1½in) pastry cutter to cut out 12 rounds. Brush the top of the cakes with the remaining marmalade, then place a jelly disc on top of each.

Place the chocolate in a microwaveable bowl and melt in 30-second bursts in the microwave, stirring between each burst. Set aside to cool for 5 minutes. Spoon a little chocolate over the top of each jelly round and leave to set.

BUTTERFLY CAKE

SERVES 16

For the cake

375g (1⅔ cups) unsalted butter, softened, plus extra for greasing

375g (1⅔ cups) golden caster (superfine) sugar

6 large eggs

375g (2½ cups) self-raising flour

3 tsp baking powder

1 tbsp vanilla extract

3–4 tbsp milk

For the buttercream

250g (1 cup, plus 2 tbsp) unsalted butter, softened

450g (3¾ cups) icing (powdered) sugar

1 tsp vanilla extract

1 tbsp milk

To decorate

icing (powdered) sugar, for dusting

500g (1lb 2oz) pale pink ready-to-roll fondant icing

4 tbsp raspberry or strawberry jam

edible gold confetti

white shimmer pearls

coloured sugar-coated chocolate buttons

pink sugar

thick strawberry laces

sugared flowers and butterflies

Preheat the oven to 180°C/350°F/gas 4. Lightly grease a deep 23cm (9in) round springform cake tin with butter and line the bottom and sides with baking paper.

Start by making the cake. Place the butter and sugar in a very large bowl and beat with an electric whisk until pale and fluffy. Add the eggs, one at a time, beating well between each addition. Alternatively, use a stand mixer.

Recipe continues overleaf

Sift over the flour and baking powder and fold in using a large metal spoon. Add the vanilla extract and enough milk for the mixture to be of a dropping consistency. If the mixture looks like it is splitting while you are adding the eggs, add 1 tbsp of the flour mix and continue as above; this should help stabilize the mixture.

Spoon the mixture into the prepared tin and smooth the top with a spatula. Bake for 1 hour, or until well risen, slightly springy to the touch and a skewer inserted into the middle of the cake comes out clean. Remove the cake from the oven, peel off the baking paper and transfer to a wire rack to cool.

Meanwhile, make the buttercream. Beat the butter, icing sugar, vanilla extract and milk in a large bowl with an electric whisk until pale and fluffy.

Dust the work surface with icing sugar, roll out the pink fondant icing to 5mm (¼in) thick and use it to cover a 30 x 40cm (12 x 16in) rectangular cake board.

Cut the cake in half horizontally and spread one cut side with the jam and the other with a little buttercream. Sandwich together, then cut in half vertically to make two semi-circles.

Cut a small triangle from the middle of the flat edges of the two semi-circles. Sandwich these two triangles of cake together and shape them into a rounded oblong to make the body of the butterfly. Cover in buttercream and an even layer of gold confetti.

Turn the two semi-circles round so that they are back to back to make the wings and place onto the middle of the cake board.

Spread buttercream all over the wings and then place the gold-covered body in the middle between the wings. Decorate the butterfly with white pearls, coloured sugar-coated chocolate buttons and pink sugar. Thread cocktail sticks into the middle of two 5cm (2in) lengths of strawberry lace and stick these into the top of the cake for antennae.

Decorate the board with sugared flowers and butterflies and serve.

TIP

This butterfly looks super impressive and yet it is really quite easy to make and doesn't require any special tins. It is better if you can make the sponge the day before as it will be easier to shape and ice. You could always pop it in the freezer for 30 minutes before you start shaping to make this process easier.

WHITE CHOCOLATE RAINBOW CAKE

SERVES 16

For the cake

350g (½ cup plus 2 tsp) unsalted butter, softened, plus extra for greasing

350g (2⅔ cups) self-raising flour, plus extra for dusting

350g (1¾ cups) golden caster (superfine) sugar

6 large free-range eggs

3 tsp baking powder

1 tablespoon vanilla extract

6 tbsp milk

6 gel food colourings (red, orange, yellow, blue, green and purple)

To decorate

300g (10½oz) white chocolate

400g (1¾ cups) unsalted butter, softened

400g (3 cups) icing (powdered) sugar

2 tsp vanilla extract

coloured sugar-coated chocolate buttons

Preheat the oven to 180°C/350°F/gas 4. Lightly grease four 20cm (8in) round non-stick shallow baking tins, add a little flour and shake so that the bottom and sides are thinly coated with flour. Shake out the excess.

Beat the butter and sugar together in a very large bowl with an electric whisk or stand-alone mixer until pale and fluffy. Add the eggs, one at a time, beating well between each addition.

Sift over the flour and baking powder and fold in using a large metal spoon. Fold in the vanilla extract and milk until the mixture is of a dropping consistency.

Recipe continues overleaf

Divide the mixture evenly between six bowls. Add about ¼ tsp of colour to each bowl so that you have six different colours of mix. The colours need to be quite vibrant as they will fade slightly during cooking.

Spoon the mixtures into four of the prepared tins (reserve the two remaining colours to bake in the next batch) and bake for 15 minutes. Swap the tins over so that all the cakes cook evenly and bake for a further 3–5 minutes. Press the tops with your finger – if they are slightly springy to the touch and the cakes have come away from the sides of the tins they should be ready.

Remove the cakes from their tins and leave to cool completely on wire racks. Wash and dry two tins, lightly grease and dust with flour as before, and fill with the remaining two cake mixtures. Smooth the tops with the back of a spoon and bake for 18–20 minutes, or until springy to the touch. Remove the cakes from their tins and leave to cool completely on wire racks.

To make the icing, place the chocolate in a microwavable bowl and melt in 30-second bursts in the microwave, stirring between each burst, then set aside. Beat together the butter and icing sugar until soft and fluffy, then pour in the melted chocolate and vanilla extract and beat until smooth.

To assemble the cake, spread a little of the icing onto a serving plate and place the purple layer on top. Spread with a little more icing and place the blue layer on top, then repeat with the green, yellow, orange and finally red layer. Spread icing over the top and sides of the cake in an even layer using a palette knife. Decorate with sugar-coated chocolate buttons in a rainbow pattern over the top and sides of the cake and serve.

INDEX

INDEX

INDEX

Cath Kidston® acknowledgements

Special thanks to everyone involved in the making of the book: to Elaine Ashton, Suzi Avens, Katie Buckingham, Sue Chidler, Caroline Dolan, Natasha Hinds- Payne, Gemma Hurley, Elisabeth Lester, Lyndsey Nangle, Romilly Smith, Elinor Turner, Jack Weaver and Andrea Yorston.

Publishing Director: Sarah Lavelle
Creative Director: Helen Lewis
Editor: Amy Christian
Designer: Gemma Hayden
Photographer: Dan Jones
Recipe writer and food stylist: Anna Burges-Lumsden
Food stylist assistants: Lou Kenny and Charlotte O'Connell
Prop stylist: Holly Bruce
Production Manager: Stephen Lang
Production Director: Vincent Smith

First published in 2017 by
Quadrille Publishing
Pentagon House
52–54 Southwark Street
London SE1 1UN
www.quadrille.co.uk

Quadrille is an imprint of Hardie Grant
www.hardiegrant.com.au

Text © 2016 Cath Kidston
All photography © 2017 Dan Jones
Design and layout © 2017 Quadrille
Publishing

Cataloguing in Publication Data: a catalogue record for this book is available from the British Library.

ISBN: 978 178713 016 6

Printed in China

For more Cath Kidston products, visit cathkidston.com